Ecclesia

Zak Landrum
Diana Small

with contributions by Dr. Randy VanderMey, Hayley Fulton
Kellie Parkinson, Ethan Warner, Andrew Massena
Ashley Myers, Becky Thompson, Justin Davis

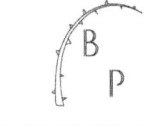

BRAMBLEWOOD PRESS, LLC
SANTA BARBARA

No part of this book may be sold or duplicated in any form, including, but not limited to, print, audio, video, or performance. All dramatic rights of this play are protected by copyright, and no performance or for profit reading, public or private, is permitted without the written consent of the author. All inquiries into such matters may be addressed to the publisher, who acts as the author's representative unless otherwise indicated.

Cover design by Taylor Gray
Interior design by Greg Wadsworth,

Copyright © Zak Landrum, 2008
All rights reserved.

A percentage of the profits of the sale of this book go toward the ongoing support of All Nations Education.

ISBN: 978-0-9797665-6-5

Bramblewood Press, LLC
729 De La Vina Street
Santa Barbara, CA 93101
www.bramblewoodpress.com

Printed in the United States of America

Zak - For the many people who brought me to a place of inspiration, and for the countless others that made this dream possible.

Diana - For the community at Westmont College, without whom there would have been no play. Thanks to my co-writer for his unabashed faith and flattery.

Contents

Director's Note	9
Author's Note	13
Note from All Nations Education	15
Cast of Characters	19
Scene 1: The Present	21
Scene 2. The Vision	23
Scene 3. Pentecost	27
Scene 4. Calling	29
Scene 5. Letters From a Prison	31
Scene 6. The Martyr	33
Scene 7. Searching for Fire	35
Scene 8. The Dance Throughout History	37
Scene 9. Apocalypse	43
Appendix A. Acknowledgments	49
Appendix B. Angel Writings	55
Appendix C. Sketches	77
Appendix E. Suggested Readings	87

Easter, 2008.

Time is a strange thing. In this moment on Easter Sunday, I write to you who are three weeks ahead of me, you who know the answer to the question I right now long to know: how will it go? These words for you (and the future me) are a window to the time I sat alone at my desk, three weeks before the simultaneous premiere and finale of *Ecclesia*.

This play is last installment of a trilogy titled *Redemption History*, a collection of theatricality that has become a way of marking time through my college experience. At its most basic, the original idea was to translate the story of the Bible into a theatrical medium, to artfully tell the story of humanity from a Christian point of view. At the time the vision struck, I had three years of college left, so it seemed to make sense to break such a big story into three parts and tell it over three years. Father, Son, Spirit. The triune imagery worked in this project's favor from the beginning.

These plays were born from the ashes of my entry into theatre, which was not that long ago. Spring of 2005, I acted in a production of *A Midsummer Night's Dream* under Dr. John Blondell's direction, where I floated in another world for six, glorious weeks. Everything in me was challenged, it seemed, as I spent hours pacing back and forth in dorm lounges memorizing out loud, diving around on stage in rehearsals as a demon fairy king, and falling nightly in love with a regal queen. When the show ended after a mere six performances, something in me snapped, grieved, awoke. Art and purpose and athleticism and spirituality and community all came into brilliant clarity in the death of this theatrical community. A burning vision came in the darkest moment of my mourning:

I needed to take this incredibly powerful way of telling stories, and tell the story most important to me. I still have the little page in my journal that has a scrawled series of pictures: a fruit offered, a cross, an empty tomb, and two curious words: "Redemption History?"

The plays have grown in size and scope as I have grown in understanding and theatrical artistry. But the opposite is true, as well: the shows have often been my teacher. Part I, simply called *Redemption History*, established the conflict by telling the Genesis 1-3 story of creation to the fall of man. In an entirely wordless piece, music, dance, movement, and technical effects spoke of the Beginning. We only had enough money to put the actors in unitards borrowed from the dance department and raise and lower sheets from the ceiling, but what we lacked in finances, we made up for with fiery spirit and creativity. I will never forget the overwhelming emotion of that final night, watching Adam and Eve waltz to a melody I first heard months before in the 2am darkness of Dean Chapel.

Redemption History II raised the bar, or changed the target, in practically every way. Instead of three chapters of text, this performance would cover 4000 years: the call of Abram to the Resurrection of Jesus. Instead of the *RH* forty-five minutes, this show ran two and a half hours. Instead of seating the audience in the house and letting them watch a play, *RHII* put them on stage with the actors and made them a part of the story. Instead of a set composed of sheets on string, we could pay for a full set and interesting costumes. And instead of a show that was simply a beautiful story to tell, *RHII* became for me a spiritual act of contrition. This show was a long, intense act of finding what it meant to call Jesus the new Israel, to re-imagine what Scripture could sound like, and to find what a modern, faithfully Christian ritual might feel like. We used theatre, the incarnational art form, to incarnate the Story.

The centerpiece of this three-year project came three quarters through this second piece. With the stories of feeding the five thousand, turning water into wine, and manna in the wilderness all theatrically converging into the Lord's Supper, Tyler, playing Christ, invited the audience to a little table. When they came, Tyler stepped out of the world of the play and said, "The body and blood of Christ, thanks be to God." In that moment, reality clashed with artifice. Icon became image. The Word became Flesh.

And now to the show which at this writing of this I've still not seen: *Redemption History III: Ecclesia*. Our task was to tell the story of the Church, from Pentecost to the Second coming of Christ. 2000 years in two hours. This time, for both my growth as an artist and the size of the content of the story, the show had to be bigger than I could dream alone. That's why I partnered with Diana, a superbly poetic playwright, to help tell the story of a Church that is "neither Jew nor Greek, slave nor free, male or female," but all one in Jesus Christ. It's also why I tried to gather as diverse a cast as possible: diverse majors, hometowns, cultures, and ethnicities. With *Ecclesia*, we are telling a grand story, something that should point to something beyond a predominantly white, middle class, American center of learning. It's why we've been so intentional about inviting the greater Santa Barbara community to this piece. It's also why I'm so excited about the partnership of this production with the young non-profit organization All Nations Education. In many ways, they are living the mission of what this piece points toward.

Ecclesia has become for me an experiment in what I'd like to do with the rest of my life. It has become a rallying point for Christian leaders and volunteers to use art as a platform for bonding a community together, bringing faith and hope to that community, and opening that community to new ways of seeing. This work stands boldly between the two worlds of respected artistic practice and the Church "morality" skits that are regularly dismissed by the established theatrical community. With this play, there is no agenda to teach a moral lesson, proselytize, or save souls, yet I am unwilling to sell out the Christian story to make a merely interesting piece of theatre. This show attempts to say 'yes' to the creation of great art while at the same time saying 'yes' to the faith that is so deeply in us. With *Ecclesia* we are reaching back to a rich tradition in the medieval mystery plays, where plays were birthed from a faith culture. Then, as now, plays were expressions of the community life. Players were the prophets for their people.

So, where do we go from here? I hope that together, we decide to keep breathing art and incarnating the story, however that looks for our lives. I hope that we never stop learning together. May we be those that live what it means to "go into all nations," proclaiming that "the kingdom of heaven is at hand." Let us live worthy of the calling we've received.

Many blessings,

Zak Landrum

I caught the dream of the project much later than Zak Landrum. In fact, when we began collaborating, *Ecclesia* was no longer a dream, but a reality that would be performed in three months. I read Zak's preliminary draft of the project in January 2008 and for three weeks we wove our imaginations together to write a play. I worked my way through Zak's mind as the director, producer, and project leader and he made space for my artistic perspectives as a theatre maker, a woman, and a fellow faith journeyer.

My hope was to make the piece a story of the Christian Church that would be completely relevant and understandable to our contemporary and specific audience. There are so many questions about the Christian heritage with which I can only answer "I don't know." When I read the stories about Pentecost, the fiery passion of martyrs, and the return of the Christ, stories where the supernatural divine makes contact with human simplicity, I expect nothing more from myself than to be baffled and confused. It makes sense that the Genesis story of creation is told the way it is; it's a simple and sweet seven day process around which I can wrap my mind, while still understanding the truths about my existence: I am made in the image of my creator, the earth has been given to me as an undeserved gift, and I have abused my privileges and am in need of a whole lot of grace. *Ecclesia* is written in a similar way. The unclear facts are wrestled with story-poetry, so that the truths of the Christian story – sacrifice, redemption, and renewal – surpass historical and theological controversy.

I confess that I did take advantage of the audience's knowledge of the "facts." *Ecclesia* was written to be a gift to Westmont College, a community that has its own faith vocabulary and communication codes. Much of the text choices were made to suit the Christian traditions of the Westmont audience and actors. During the process, we asked fellow students questions about their theatrical tastes and several actors wrote their own convictions for the piece. *Ecclesia* was written for Westmont College to be performed in the spring of 2008. However, it is thrilling to know that it does not stop there. It is a great offering that other productions can provide in putting forth new perspectives. After all, it's not a completed story that Zak and I wrote; it's one that will continue to mature and transform. I am positive that much of the text of the play will have a very different meaning in a future time and community. *Ecclesia* needs to redevelop alongside the development of the Christian story.

I am blessed to have been able to write for such a project; to be a voice on behalf of the Saints that have come before me. Writing *Ecclesia* allowed me to grapple with the messy truths of my Christian heritage and this is my hope for its audiences. For the Christian Church to know itself by these stories is truly a gift. *Ecclesia* was written to encourage faith communities to live in these stories and make new ones fueled by love. It is Zak and my hope that this play be a source of inspiration for that ever-constant Christian pilgrimage.

Diana Small

After attending a rigorous, Christian liberal arts college like Westmont, I have grown to realize firsthand that higher education is absolutely necessary for human flourishing. I've studied rhetoric and communication, economics and business, philosophy and science, English and art, sociology and religion, not merely to become a fountain of facts, but instead to "expand my capacity to love." I am convinced that education liberates individuals, communities and nations from the prison of illiteracy, and acts as one of the greatest forces against poverty and injustice. All Nations Education yearns for all people to experience this kind of holistic education.

All Nations Education devotes itself to providing college-age young adults in developing countries with the resources to pursue higher education, the mentorship to become moral leaders, and the social network to pursue sustainable economic and political development.

Ecclesia is a superb expression of what is possible with a liberal arts education. It promotes a broad understanding of the world, fosters a profound sense of community, and respectfully welcomes people from all backgrounds, as it tells the story of humanity from a Christian perspective. It is my hope that as All Nations Education develops, it can help to make these kind of liberal arts projects possible for people all over the world.

Josh Daneshforooz
All Nations Education
President and Founder

Ecclesia

ORIGINAL CAST
Angel 1: Hayley Fulton
Angel 2: Kellie Parkinson
Angel 3: Ethan Warner
Angel 4: Andrew Massena
Angel 5: Ashley Myers
Angel 6: Becky Thompson
Angel 7: Justin Davis
Saints: The Westmont Gospel Choir
Priest: Rev. William B. Nelson
John: Nolan Hamlin
Mary: Geriece Jenkins
Bride: Christianne Davis
Peter: Christopher Martinez
Paul: Andrew Massena
Stephen: Justin Davis
Jesus: Tyler Leivo
Satan: Ian Redford

ORIGINAL MUSICIANS:
Piano and vocal: Allyson Arendsee
Vocal: Allison Sylva
Cello: Benjamin Vander Wall
Double Bass: Matt Kissel
Violin: Rachel Mertensmeyer
Organ: Matthew Roy

ORIGINAL CREW:
Chief Designer: Matt Jones
Graphic Design/Electronic Music Composition: Taylor Gray
Orchestral Music Composition: Landon Strine and Greg Wadsworth
Videography: Nathanael Matanick
Master Electrician: Toby Lounsbury
Costume Design/Construction: Matt Jones, Lynne Martens, and Sara Ziegler
Make Up Design: Hayley Fulton
Stage Manager: Suzy Galletly
Business Manager: Eric Jen
Technical Support: Garcia Work, Michael Aguilar, Austin Ward, Kim Crawford, Dave Tetrick, Evan Pollard, Kelsey White, Julia Johnson, Chelsea Sleeth

Ecclesia

	CAST OF CHARACTERS
ANGELS	Seven prophet poets. They are the wisest people you know – your grandfather, fourth grade teacher, older sister – with the roughness and audacity of a liquor store clerk. They have fully invaded the human experience while maintaining their celestial perspective. They transcend time, space, and physical form.
SAINTS	Statues of all the Christian martyrs. Their prayers are songs. Mary is their choir leader.
PRIEST	The leader of the service. He is liturgical yet contemporary. He makes sense of the poetry of prophets while speaking words of forefathers like they are his own. He is the battle-hardened old man that every one loves, but has a sorcerer's power that burns from his eyes.
JOHN	The author of Revelation and an island exile. He's nervous company for himself and can barely distinguish reality from illusion. John's human flesh cannot contain his divine experiences; he has become earthy, stripped of civilized conduct.
MARY	The mother of Christ and the leader of the saints. She is the choral leader whose regal song guides the Bride through her journey.
BRIDE	She is a recently engaged young woman. Completely in love, she is also naïve, compulsive, and vengeful.
PETER	A disciple of Christ and eye witness to the birth of the church during Pentecost. He is like a love drunk father stumbling out of the delivery room. He is also the young version of the Priest.
PAUL	A prisoner in chains. Paul is the man forced to share his murderous past to prevent others from making his mistakes. He is a Pharisee turned outlaw, riches to rages, but still has intellectual habits.
STEPHEN	The first Christian martyr. He is a man of the people, a wilderness prophet working in urban slums. Stephen has a ferocity and strength harnessed in gentleness and patience.
JESUS	The groom waiting for his bride. His power is in his fidelity and undying love.
SATAN	A lying, cheating, hypocrite. The boy on the playground who pulls girl's hair, the woman who cuts in line at the grocery store, the oil tycoon who can weasel his way out of any illegality. He is his own greatest audience and has the power to annoy, but completely convince. He is the voice in your head that keeps you up at night.

Scene 1: The Present

A priest stands on top of a golden ziggurat covered in prayer. He looks ready to begin a service of worship. Seven street prophets slam down prayers. A choir of saints softly sing a hymn. We begin.

Priest. (*Sings*)

Veni Sancte Spiritus	(Come, thou Holy Spirit, come,
Et emitte caelitus	And from thy celestial home
Lucis tuae radium	Shed thy light and brilliancy)
O lux beatissima,	(O thou Light, most pure and blest,
Reple cordis intima	Shine within the inmost breast
Tuorum fidelium	Of thy faithful company.)
Da tuis fidelibus,	(Fill the faithful, who confide
In te confidentibus,	In thy power to guard and guide,
Sacrum septenarium.	With thy sev'nfold Mystery.
Amen.	Amen.)

(*Speaks*) To this sacred place, our Holy Cathedral, I welcome you in the name of the Father, the Son, and the Holy Spirit. Amen. Please pray with me:

> God of power,
> May the boldness of your spirit transform us,
> may the gentleness of your Spirit lead us,
> and may the gifts of your Spirit equip us
> to serve and worship you now and always. Amen.

John. Seven lamp stands, seven stars, lights, angels, fire, words, beings, letters. Seven lamp stands, seven stars, lights, angels, fire, words, beings, letters...

Scene 2. The Vision

John. Seven lamp stands, seven stars, lights....Do not leave me on this island. Stars, lights, angels, fire, words, beings, letters, words. Yes, I see you, but why do you look at me? You came with clouds, I have ink. Yes, take hold, it's burning my fingers, eyes, schedules, nightmares, mouth. How can I speak on your behalf? I am not worthy. I am not worthy. I am not worthy. Who am I? I am not worthy. Have mercy on a sinner. I am not worthy. Write? Now. Use me as you will. Get me down from here. Blessed is the one who reads the words of this prophecy, and blessed are those who hear it and take to heart what is written in it, because the time is near. Sshh. Don't kill the messenger.

> The sound of power grows. The street prophets become warriors of the celestial realm. These angels form a frozen tableau of what's to come.

There! Seven lamp stands. Seven stars. Lights. Fire. Words. Beings. Letters. Angels. I see them! Omnipotent Being. The eyes rip me from this world. The feet send roots into the ground. The skin, blinding bronze. Hair white as the sun. And the words, the words were thunder, but melted into honey. (*John listens, then writes.*) "The seven lamp stands are the seven churches. The seven stars are angels, the spirits, the voices of these churches. The voices of my bride, he says. The voices of my BRIDE." He says, "She is not ready to see my face. Write to her. Give her my voice."

The angels prepare for their address.

Angels. Holy, Holy, Holy is the Lord God Almighty.
Holy, Holy, Holy is the Lord God Almighty.
Holy, Holy, Holy is the Lord God Almighty.

ANGEL 1. Father in Heaven, the power of your spirit may fall once in a generation or once in living memory on your prophets - men, women, even children -

ANGEL 2. Not fortune tellers,

ANGEL 3. not foretellers,

ANGEL 4. but FORTHTELLERS.

Angel 5. Speakers of your Word, your difficult, simple, costly, priceless, life-transforming word of peace into the human muddle,

ANGEL 6. into the social sea of boiled oil and the stakes of human anger,

ANGEL 7. into the fire of blinded accusation.

JOHN. Your Son, Jesus Christ, who spoke forth that word and was, in the flesh, that Word, told those who took offense at him:

ANGELS. Prophets have no place in their own country and in their own house. Prophets have no place in their own country and in their own house. Prophets have no place in their own country and in their own house.

ANGEL 1. And so tonight, if this is our house and if WE

ANGEL 2. WE are the seven spirits of supernatural PROPHECY

ANGEL 3. PROPHECY made flesh so that you can be made to believe. IF WE

ANGEL 4. IF WE are the angels of the seven churches, imaginations' hopes and dreams given life in this reality, it would SEEM

Angel 5. SEEM that you should just tune out! Walk away! CURSE the prophets that come in His name! Get your money back and live your normal Sunday. But I INVITE YOU to follow me while we breathe a different way.

ANGEL 7. JESUS Christ, the blazing God of STEEL skin, white lightning, and liquid thunder voice commands you to BE the BRIDE that is ready to BE SEEN. WE are those churches, who spit fire while our Spirit Swords gleam the bold light of Christ's Life. But, GOD!

ANGEL 6. I ask you, on behalf of all to whom we are appearing:

Angels. What have we become?

ANGEL 6. We were the fire of the good news that couldn't be leashed by tongue, trade, deed or creed.

ANGEL 5. We were bold, communion eaters and drinkers of the Righteous One.

ANGELS. Now?

ANGEL 5. We stumble into church Sunday morning and wash out last night's hangover with communion bread and blood.

ANGEL 2. We forgive the pastor his pornographic frenzy and banish the unmarried teen and her protruding belly.

ANGELS. What have we become?

ANGEL 3. We were the Bride who prepared herself in the inner chamber of the Holy of Holies. We were carriers of the church.

ANGEL 7. We shot forth from the vine and curled our way into every dark space. We listened to the whispers and silenced the arrogant.

ANGEL 5. We touched the untouchables. We spoke the unbelievable. The unknown clutched tightly to our breast.

ANGEL 2. We were walkers of the Way. We never stopped moving towards that day. The last day.

ANGELS. And now?

ANGEL 4. We beg Christ his return, but give him a schedule: after I am rich, before I am wrinkled, between fortune and frailty -- but still, Jesus, come.

ANGEL 6. In haste, two girls gather under the guise of accountability to relate over common struggles with sexual sin. But instead of drawing each other up and out, they just wallow in their common guilt.

ANGEL 7. At the coffee shop, I saw a pretty, young woman walk through the door. There, in my mind, I undressed her. Before long, I dashed into the bathroom to finish the job. Then I returned to my seat with clean hands, run under the water with soap.

ANGEL 3. A prominent church in the middle of Vienna, California sends out a letter to its congregation stating that the youth pastor had been asked to leave because of a relationship he had with a girl in the youth group. Two months later, the congregation receives a second letter. One of the head pastors had been asked to leave for having an affair.

ANGEL 2. We've become a church that is divided, broken, and dissected. In Santa Barbara alone, there are fifty-one churches and counting.

ANGELS. What have we become?

ANGEL 7. These sins have brought us, angels of the churches, the seven spirits of God, to our knees.

ANGEL 1. We are in need. Cornered in Crisis. And so we say GOD!

ANGEL 4. Distract us from what is popular.

ANGEL 6. Make our hearts beat to the rhythm of your words, your heart.

ANGEL 7. Your embers, your love.

ANGEL 1. Help us remember when we lived liked passionate fools.

ANGEL 5. When the flames from our fingers were guides for the lost. Help us live this beginning.

ANGELS. Beginning.

SCENE 3. PENTECOST

PRIEST. The Lord be with you.
SAINTS. And also with you.
PRIEST. A reading from the Holy Gospel according to Luke:
SAINTS. Glory to you, Lord.
PRIEST. When the day of Pentecost came, they were all with one mind in one place. And suddenly from heaven there came a sound like the rush of mighty wind, and it filled the entire house where they were sitting. Divided tongues, as of fire, appeared among them, and settled on each of them. All of them were filled with the Holy Spirit and began to speak in other tongues. Languages, as the Spirit gave them utterance.

The Angels have made a small house. Mary circles the house slowly.

ANGEL 1. She was born in a small house. Hands and feet and faith were bursting from the seams. Children stuck tight in corners, guarded by the arms of their mothers. Men and their sandals firm against the windows and doors. He had only been gone forty days, but the right hand in heaven seemed to be an awfully far off place. Sweat sang to the dirt floor and chapped lips could utter no words. The cry from the womb of the creator came as a shock. Unexpected. There was no time for ice chips or anesthesia. Who would be the one to catch the child? To rub birthing ankles and wipe fear off her forehead? Mary's voice did all the work. *Mary begins to sing the Magnificat.* It rocked the daughter from heaven's imagination and placed her in the hands of humans. She was born. We were born. Together in one place. Together in one fire.

The bride emerges from the small house. She is blazing.

ANGELS. Glory be to Jesus Christ, our Lord and King, Victor over death!

The angels's words are heard in a thousand tongues. The saints tongues are lit on fire. Images from other countries. Faces and flags. Maps and flames.

ANGELS AND SAINTS. Hail Mary, full of grace, the Lord is with you. Blessed are you among women, and blessed is the fruit of your womb, Jesus. Holy Mary, Mother of God, pray for us sinners now and at the hour of death. Amen.

MARY. *Speaking to the Bride.* The Lord said unto me, "Before I formed you in the belly I knew you; and before you came out of the womb I sanctified you, and I ordained you to be a prophet unto the nations." Then I said, "Lord GOD! I cannot speak: for I am just a child." But the Lord said to me, "Say not, 'I am a child': for you will go to all that I will send to you, and what ever I command, you shall speak. Be not afraid of their faces: for I am here to deliver you." Then with His hand, the Lord touched my mouth. And He said to me, "Behold, I have put my words in your mouth. See, on this day I have placed you over the nations and over the kingdoms, to root out, and to pull down, and to destroy, and to throw down, to build, and to plant."

Scene 4. Calling

PRIEST. Please join me as we affirm our faith in the words of the Apostle's Creed:

PRIEST, ANGELS AND SAINTS. I believe in God, the Father Almighty, the Creator of heaven and earth, and in Jesus Christ, His only Son, our Lord:

> Who was conceived of the Holy Spirit, born of the Virgin Mary, suffered under Pontius Pilate, was crucified, died, and was buried.
> He descended into hell.
> The third day He rose from the dead.
> He ascended into heaven and sits at the right hand of God the Father Almighty, whence He shall come to judge the living and the dead.
>
> I believe in the Holy Spirit, the holy catholic church, the communion of saints, the forgiveness of sins, the resurrection of the body, and life everlasting.

Amen.

PETER. All of you, brothers and sisters in Jerusalem, listen to what I've got to say! Don't be fooled. No one here is drunk. It's the third hour of the day for heaven's sakes. No. I, Peter, the apostle, can explain it with only the anticipated unbelievable. It was predicted by the prophet Joel, so long ago. Her arrival should not be a shock. God told Joel about this very day. The day she would be born! He said sons and daughters would prophesy. Young men would see visions. Old men would dream dreams. Joel warned us of the wonders. The blood and fire and clouds of smoke. A black sun and red moon. Today God has poured his spirit upon our flesh, men and women alike, so that we will prophesy. Come in and look at her. She is yours. She is you. Call on the name of Lord and you will be saved!

ANGELS AND SAINTS. Call on the name of the Lord.

ANGELS. Christ, King, Lord, Master, Ruler, Shepherd, Lamb, Child, Widow, is the same Servant, Healer, Teacher, Forgiver, Deliverer, Sufferer, Warrior, Peacemaker.

ANGEL 6. Who gives us the grace we need to survive.

ANGEL 4. Who gives us the grace we need to shut our eyes, reach out our hands, and grab for the rescue we know is there.

ANGELS AND SAINTS. Come rescue me!

ANGEL 1. But it won't look like salvation unless you close your eyes and search with faith.

ANGEL 2. And when we are faithful we will be put on SPIKES, burned at STAKES, FLAYED alive. Our mothers will SPIT on us and our fathers will abandon our name. We will become IGNORED, ISOLATED, FORGOTTEN. We won't know our own, bloody faces.

PRIEST. The cries of the saints ring out from under the altar, pleading for justice. Beloved, we do not think of a martyr simply as a good Christian who has been killed because that person just happens to be a Christian. Nor do we think of martyrs simply as good Christians who have been elevated to the company of the Saints. The true martyr is the one who has become the instrument of God, who has lost his or her will in the will of God, and who no longer desires anything for personal gain, not even the glory of being a martyr. And beloved, saints are not made by accident.

The saints are lit. They become stained glass statues. Stephen is remembered.

The Lord be with you.

SAINTS. And also with you.

PRIEST. A reading from the letters of Saint Paul:

Scene 5. Letters From a Prison

PAUL. I write light, wrapped in chain and stone, and with all these adornments I am still nothing more than a slave. Stripped of all that I have, of everything I used to be. And I thank God every day for it. I used to live with my eyes opened wide. I was too afraid of walking into walls and being wrong. The things I saw myself doing. I hope the Lord gives you wisdom and shows you truth. My eyes had to be burned to uselessness, I pray that you catch on faster than I did. Stop looking ahead. See what is right in front of you. You are His body, the church. Your hands can be His hands. Your eyes, His eyes. Your heart, His heart. The union you have with Christ, is like that of a marriage. Remember that as the Church, you are the Bride of Christ, His most beautiful creation.

The Magnificat plays again. Paul's letters are sent and an execution procession begins.

I want to make sure that you understand that I'm not Christ. I'm the man who has been forgiven. Rescued from killing you and myself. I want to make sure that you understand that I'm a murderer. Stephen. He was first, and after him, hundreds of others. I murdered them; I murdered you and myself. I've been rescued, but these chains are more than iron. I don't want to remember, help me remember.

Scene 6. The Martyr

Stephen stands holding one stone. His execution swirls around him. His faith does not waver.

STEPHEN. How do I know who I am? How do I know where I've been? I own my speech no more than this stone. Forgive them Father, they know not what they do. There is a place on my mother's thighs, where our stories are hidden. They were written there long ago; when the rocking of her arms were strong enough to soothe my small frame. I would put my ear against her lap and listen to the words of Abraham and Joseph, Moses and David. The prophets. Forgive them Father, they know not what they hear. There is a point on that mountain and a vein in all the leaves that soak straight to the rays of the angels. They are fire, crystallized. Burning through the rock and the gold and the temples. Forgive them Father, they know not what they see. There is an incense. Turning through this very room. It sneaks through our eyes and swims to our blood, boiling the love of our Deliverer. Pushing our bones to go and be my body. Forgive them Father, they know not what they feel. There is a woman, naked and torn on the sidewalk. She is my mother, my teacher, she is you. She cries for a touch, a smile, a story, but I am dead. Won't you? Will others? I am not the fire! Pass this flame to another. Plant new seeds from my branches. Will your son's story continue or will we give up? Forgive them Father, they know not what they will become.

Stephen stains the Bride with blood and the song Swing Low, Sweet Chariot ceremoniously carries him away.

PRIEST. And thus on earth the Church mourns and rejoices at once, in a fashion that the world cannot understand; so in Heaven the Saints are most high, having made themselves most low, and are seen, not as we see them, but in the light of the Godhead from which they draw their being.

Saints own their names.

Scene 7. Searching for Fire

Angels. So where are the martyrs among us?

Angel 1. We're called Saints, but do we dare compare ourselves to Stephen? The one who BLED TRUTH to the very last drop.

Angel 3. The one who LOVED his enemies to the very LAST STONE.

Angel 6. The one who had the FIRE to the very last GOD WORK.

Angel 5. STEPHEN'S BLAZING TONGUE left trails of miracles in alleyways, sick houses and secret places in the corners of mountains. The Church fed upon the burning blood of martyrs, was purified in the passion of her persecution, and loved in that labor.

Angels. So where is that fire among us?

Angel 4. That fire now is up the single road in the Down, where the walls of St. John's Abby hold inexplicable splendor of every faith's expressions, symbols. I saw the Benedictine priest before the altar, giving the body to anyone who came forward, down the aisle. To anyone who came, he gave them our Lord.

Angel 1. THAT FIRE IS the church for rockabilly and goths called the Church for Sinners. There people who lead alternative life styles can worship without fear of social alienation. All people are welcome.

Angel 2. THAT FIRE IS a plastic bag of razors surrendered, pressed into the palm of a listener. Scars that are revealed, rubbed with lotion, wept over and kissed, as freedom is finally found.

Angels. So where is that fire among us?

Angel 3. That fire drifted into the church of St. Boniface in San Francisco with each homeless person who comes through the door. Ever-welcome, ever-open, she finds an empty pew in the twilight light of the cathedral, a place to rest the head, surrounded by icons and statues of saints long past. Christ hangs on the cross at the altar, nailed on high with the beggars of the world at his feet.

Angel 6. That fire fuels the feet of shoeless children in the dawn, as they crawl forth, unprompted, to hear a missionary's song.

Angel 5. That fire bleeds from weeping eyes of a new mother, adopting a child that is not her own.

Angel 2. That fire is a child being the first to learn to read in her home, her class, her village.

Angels. So where is that fire among us?

Angel 4. Our mouths can't get through breakfast without tearing the truth apart. We bashfully hiccup smoke because we're embarrassed to admit that there's nothing left inside of our cages, but charcoal.

Angel 1. Our lukewarm Bible study tea times have made us lazy, outdated, and winded. We're a closet full of excuses dressed as holy pursuit.

Angels. The Bride is now: Cold. Weak. Broken. Bereft.

Angel 7. Look at yourself. Is this what you call preparation? So where is that fire now?

Priest. Through the Holy Spirit, Jesus breathed life into the Church just as He breathed life into Adam in the beginning. From the moment of Pentecost, forty days after His glorious ascension, Jesus has been preparing us for the day of His return. By blessing us with His Spirit, He gave the believers access to His power and His divine authority. He invested His power in us. In fallen humanity.

Scene 8. The Dance Throughout History

Music and film. Saints charge to welcome Christ. Jesus enters. He proposes to the Bride and she accepts. A lovers' kiss. Jesus gives Priest's scripture to Bride as a parting gift.

PRIEST. The flames of which Stephen spoke, the fire that consumed his every fear, has burned for centuries since. It birthed the Church, gave the prophetic eye to the souls of God's children. It allowed every tongue to speak of the Great Goodness of Christ's sacrifice and the Great Majesty of His Resurrection. And suddenly from heaven there came a sound like the rush of mighty wind, and it filled the entire house where they were sitting. Divided tongues, as of fire, appeared among them, and settled on each of them.

ANGEL 7. 64 Anno Domini. She accepted Christ's proposal, he lit her mouth on fire. The bride danced in fiery passion for her Savior. The Romans feared the Christian inferno and did what they could to keep the flames from spreading. Brothers and sisters accused of incestuous marriage were the first to take the heat. Fueled by her love for Christ, the Bride refused to resist torture. The Roman streets lit like madness with the silent screams of burning men and women.

Saints are tortured, beaten, crucified.

ANGEL 4. Christians were dressed with the hides of beasts then chased by dogs. They were nailed to crosses, set aflame, and when the daylight passed away, they became night time lamps.

Saints are massacred.

ANGEL 5. She was tempted with power and money, but she would be faithful. She looked to her Groom's love letters. They kept her on the straight and narrow. In 303 AD, Diocletian orders the last and greatest persecution of Christians to date in the Roman Empire: "There will be no engagement, give over your book stupid girl!" Strong and rebellious in all the right ways, she refuses. She must wait for the return of her Groom.

ANGEL 2. But sometimes, she does get lonely and needs are needs. When tactics change, she trades the book for a date, a slow dance, a kiss...

She gives the Book to Rome, her new lover. He starts ripping pages from the Book.

And how do you think that makes her martyr friends feel? Pushed aside for a Friday night fling? She's not only a traitor, but the Bride-to-be is a two-faced liar.

ANGEL 1. One part of her clings to the feet of her Father while the other half is making out at the movies. Ten years later the film is over and she's ready to come home. What to do, what to do?

ANGELS. Unity or purity? Who are you church?

Angel 2. 312 AD. Constantine ends the brutal persecution, but the peace comes at a hidden price. The Bride must become Roman. He clothes her in a concubine's dress of death and statehood. She becomes irresistible, and when she thinks Christ's not looking, she sneaks into Rome's bedroom. The Pope, her glorious head, is now imprisoned by the politics of the Prince of this world. Her Roman lover traffics her into service of the state and pays her with tolerance. Soon this isn't enough. The Prince always wants more.

The Brides affair with Rome becomes passionately intense.

Angel 6. It's in 392 that her affair with the State is made PUBLIC. It's her choice; she can't hide the bulging belly for long. She gives birth to hybrid children who don't even recognize one another: Christian Romans, Christian Byzantines then European Christians, and Asian Christians.

ANGEL 4. But, amidst the chaos, she bestows her purity in her precious newborns, the monks. She hides them in convents and islands, hoping they'll later save their brothers and sisters.

ANGELS. Unity or purity?

ANGEL 7. 400 years later and Charlemane compels her to crown him holy. She can barely tell the difference between the bed she shares with Rome and the ring she still wears on her finger. Power clenched in her bleeding fists she rallies her children for war. It was a family reunion that will always be remembered.

ANGEL 2. Drunk with arrogance, brothers and sisters raised swords and praised their mother for all she had done. The not-so-chaste bride made a toast to her children, numb in a bloody-drunk coma:

Ecclesia

ANGEL 1. "Drink up, my Christian warriors: You've been so eager to fight for the legacy of your mother, well here's your chance. For too long you've been bullied and pushed around, but it's time you stood up for your family. Remember, Christ has made us a promise and we must show him we're in it 'til death do we part! Go and fight for the deliverance of the holy places, the pride of your mother's name. Go and merit an eternal reward. And if you are conquered, you will have the glory of dying in the very same place as Jesus Christ, and God will never forget that He found you in the holy battalions. If you must have blood, bathe in the blood of the infidels. Soldiers of hell, become soldiers of the living God!"

ANGEL 2. The Crusades lasted for centuries. "GOD WILLS IT!" was the battle cry.

Bride becomes Athena rallying troops for battle as the saints splatter her with blood.

ANGEL 7. They ride for liberation, immortality, freedom - ready to kill their Arab rivals. The dark-skinned infidels must be destroyed. The bride is now a mother of war.

ANGEL 4. Yet still the monks are hiding. Their prayers keep the promise-fire burning. They rewrite and illuminate the love letters their mother has given them for safe-keeping.

ANGELS. Unity or purity?

Angel 5. Then comes the break-up. 1052 years old and Rome says it's over. Ripped. Torn. Eastern Church. Western Church. Greek Orthodox versus Latin Catholic. Their children don't know whose side to take. It's heartbreaking, but let's be honest, after centuries of fighting, it was an emotionless romance anyway.

ANGEL 1. The law-suit settles in her favor. She is more opulent than ever and only growing more powerful, so her new lover, the Prince of Darkness, tells her. But naturally, the children warriors are confused. Soldiers from the West are killing other Christians from the East, mistaking them for enemies. Two popes, then three, claim authority. 1377. The Great Western Schism. Who to trust?

Bride's dress is ripped significantly

ANGEL 4. The monks emerge with education and hope for a brighter future. They come to their mother and she turns them into money. Create Stability! Create culture! Capitalize! Make yourself a part of the land! Renaissance. Art. Buildings. Money. 1500 years in the making and she is:

ANGELS. Power. Art. Indulgences. Money. Stone. Wood. Carved.

Angel 7. The steps of the cathedral are concrete tongues against his frail feet, flowing over gray pavement.

NAILS upon the steps of the cathedral-hallowed morning

NAILS into the hearts of those who've passed this way before.

NAILS blood upon cathedral's door.

ANGEL 6. In 1521, Luther finds her and hammers her faults to her breast. "Here I stand, I can do no other," and she's broken. Again! Ripped. Who is she now? The Pro-test-ants shatter her personality, her aging face has lost its seductive powers. A mid-life crisis sends stained glass screaming in a thousand directions. She must make it up to the Groom somehow.

ANGEL 4. 1540. The Jesuits fight back for Catholicism. They leave to start anew in other cultures. 150 years of Catholic mission. Millions are slain in South America as she rushes in with scripture in one hand and disease in the other. Asia shares in her blessing as she tries harder than ever to find what it means to translate her purest parts to other countries.

ANGEL 6. Followed by another 150 years of the Protestant reaction, she stumbles her way into the imperialization of other countries, insisting that the crusades are over.

ANGEL 3. Fast forward.

Satan enters, dressed for a wedding. He swoons the Bride and she falls for it.

ANGEL 1. She says allegiance to governments and watches Hitler march, Stalin slaughter, and Mao murder. She watches as the greatest number of martyrs to date are killed with poison gas, machetes, and guns.

ANGEL 5. She's trying so hard to be His Bride, but she's tired, worn out, and lonely all over again. Where are you Jesus? She hides behind the Prince of this world and satisfies herself with his lies. She's got nothing left to protect. Her love for the saints is burnt out. Her heart arrests as seals are broken and bowls of judgment are poured out. She's caught in her own dirty sheets.

Bride crumbles into helpless, pitiable creature. Four angels pour out silver bowls of judgement onto the ziggurat. Blood should be dripping down the sides of the structure.

JOHN. The lion that prowls, waiting to devour, sees the church for the weak, helpless, lazy, ignorant whore that she's become. And he is near to her. Waiting for her to give birth.

Scene 9. Apocalypse

Satan is an inspiring mess: filthy yet suave, scattered yet articulate, hypocritical yet convincing.

SATAN. Did God really say you must not eat from any tree in the Garden? For God knows that when you eat of it, your eyes will be opened and you will be like God, knowing Good and Evil, right? She ate. He ate. They hid and hid and hid, but God banished them from the Garden of Eden. Stay alert! Watch out for liars and thieves and politicians and accountants and journalists and florists and the little old lady who teaches Sunday School. Your great enemy, the devil prowls around like a roaring lion, looking for someone to devour. Bread rolls and trout on the house! How did He do that? If you are the son of God tell these stones to become loaves of bread. The mouth of God? Oh, you've got me there! But what about Lazarus? You just let him die and his sisters drown in their own sorry snot. A resurrection? Didn't see that one coming! Distraction! Sexy biceps, long, long legs, kill and conquer. Take one last, long look back and you'll be salt in my broth. Second chances? You've got to be kidding me! The day of the Lord is coming. Scoffers will come, mockers will spit at the truth. We'll follow our own helpless human desires. Question: What's really going to happen when Jesus comes again? I'm getting impatient. Let's get this party started! Everything around us is going to be destroyed. Including you because you are a hypocrite and a liar. Because the things you do when you're all alone are not ignored. God sees them all and He'll take no excuses. He's the holy Lord, damn it! Do you think you can compete with that. Only perfection is allowed at His table, and believe me you're just as far from it as I am. Love rescues cats from trees. It changes diapers and helps you forget just how insignificant you are. As the scripture says, "all is meaningless." You do read your Bibles, don't you? But love can't save lives. Call your Jesus right now. Nothing's gonna' happen. Nothing ever does. It's a joke! It's all one giant game of pretend. You're wasting your time.

Shofars. Jesus gets battle ready. Angels go to war.

JOHN. I saw an angel coming down out of heaven. One hand held the key, held the key to the Abyss. He held a great chain in the other. The dragon was seized. That ancient serpent, devil, Satan, was bound. He was nailed and stoned and boiled and burned for a thousand years. The abyss crumbled over him. He would deceive the nations no longer. For one thousand. One thousand. One thousand years.

In captivity, Satan grows more powerful. He consumes his prison.

The thousand ends and Satan was released and exploded to the four corners of the earth. Dressed in lies he gathered Gog and Magog for battle.

Verses 1 and 3 of "Let All Mortal Flesh Keep Silence" begins floating through the room as the Angel of Light marches on the throne of God, slaying all angels in his path. Jesus summons his army of Saints.

The feet, billions in pairs, marched to the ends of the earth to the refuge of God's beloved.

Christ, in full view of his army, crushes the head of the Serpent.

Then fire, flames, sheets of sharp heat, flew from heaven. The devil was thrown into a lake, sulfur burning, burning, burning of beasts and false prophets. Day and night, day and night, day and night they are plagued by the fire, for ever and ever. And they are silenced. Forgotten.

The angels are reborn.

A new heaven and new earth wrap its arms around the deceased, sinking its life into the genesis roots. They soak up all the tears until the sea has vanished.

Verse 2 of "Let All Mortal Flesh Keep Silence." Jesus offers the sacraments to the Bride, she accepts. The Bride and Jesus kiss.

I see the Holy City, a new Jerusalem, bursting from Heaven. She is a bride, striking and magnificent, made new for her husband. The seven angels speak:

ANGELS. I invite you to see the Bride, the wife of the Lamb.

Verse 3 of "Let All Mortal Flesh Keep Silence." The Angels bow in submission.

JOHN. He says, I am the Alpha and the Omega, the Beginning and the End. I'll give you water when you're thirsty and it's not going to cost you a thing. I'm your Creator and you are my child. *John gives the Bible, once abused by the Bride, and returns it to the priest.* He sends His saints and angels before Him. They scream, "CHURCH."

ANGELS AND SAINTS. CHURCH, in His Name.

ANGELS. Be free from the power of the Prince of this world.

ANGELS AND SAINTS. CHURCH, in His Name.

ANGELS. Love without limits. Touch the untouchables.

ANGELS AND SAINTS. CHURCH, in His Name.

ANGELS. Be grace. Live as fire.

PRIEST. God of power,
>May the boldness of your Spirit transform us,
>May the gentleness of your Spirit lead us,
>And may the gifts of your Spirit equip us
>To serve and worship you now and always. Amen

(end)

Appendices

Every production has its own life. If ever this play is produced outside of this community, I hope the director, the cast, the technical crew, and all others who are involved with the piece use the text as a springboard for their own theatrical exploration. What follows are artifacts of what made our production of the play our production of the play: notes to thank the key players, the writings of our prophet poets, design sketches from our chief designer, and books that were helpful along the way. These pages are signposts of remembrance along what has been our journey through *Ecclesia*. May they help you along your way.

Appendix A

Acknowledgments

For years now, this project has been an experiment in giving. These people have given extravagantly to the Redemption History series, and especially this installment.

LYNETTE BENSON: Thank you for choosing to see this play for what it could be and believing in that vision. With the financial support you have provided, you perhaps more than anyone else, are the reason that so many are holding this text and will remember April 13th, 2008.

MITCHELL THOMAS: You have been constantly supportive and infinitely patient. It was from you that I learned how to carefully listen for inspiration. And thank you for continually putting up with the ravings of a madman.

JONATHAN HICKS: You've been in the trenches since the beginning. None of these shows could have happened without your many hours of labor, and your reluctant but willing hours away from Adrienne. So thank you too, Adrienne, for letting him help.

JOHN BLONDELL: With Midsummer, you opened my eyes to the theatrical world. You have since been a marvelous guide. I will always be deeply grateful.

TELFORD WORK: I think your Doctrine class enraged the Christian in me enough to spark a theological show. Nice work. Thanks for being a source of spiritual wisdom in the storm of these years, and thanks, too for championing the show in the administration.

HELEN RHEE: Thank you for all the long talks in your office that helped us get the dates right.

BRAD ELLIOT: You could easily have left us to our own means to figure things out, but instead have been a source of grace and energy and willingness. Thank you for your help in bringing these shows to life.

GREG WADSWORTH: Thanks for making publication possible. You've extended the lifespan of this show considerably.

MATT JONES: You've put your time, your blood, and yourself into each piece of armor, each staff, each sketch. It's almost inhuman how much you've accomplished in so short a time. You've blessed many people with your art. I am so thankful for your partnership in this project.

MICHAEL CONRAD II: Compatriot. You've been there since the beginning, and you've lived it all with me. Your structures have been the worlds where mystery comes to dwell.

TAYLOR GRAY: I will never forget the Adam and Eve waltz in Dean Chapel. You are *most* talented, and it has been my honor to make art with you over these last three years. Thanks for seeing it through, even in the dark times of too much to do and looming deadlines.

GERIECE JENKINS: I think you saw how huge *Ecclesia* could be before even I did. Thank you for the trust that said "yes" before I knew what I was asking. Your prayerful leadership of the Choir has been a spiritual anchor for this show.

NATHANAEL MATANICK: Thank you for pausing your insane life outside Westmont to come get involved up on the hill. Your skill is most impressive, and this whole community has been blessed by what you've given.

SUZY GALLETLY: Your faithfulness to fill any gap and go any distance has been a constant source of inspiration. Thank you for your commitment to show up even when it wasn't clear what was needed or how you could help. In that consistency, you have woven yourself into the core of this project. I am most grateful.

LEAH BENSON: A phenomenal dancer, a better friend. Thank you for allowing yourself to be Satan version 1.0, and then over the next two years becoming our champion in the scheduling wing of Westmont. Creating art with you over the last three years has been a total blessing.

LYNNE MARTENS: You've been there for the whole journey. Thanks for weathering the storms of uncertainty and long hours in the shop to make an epic project possible.

CORY SCHOOLLAND: You've collected the hundreds of images that open portals back to glorious moments. I'm deeply thankful for helping us to remember where we've been.

DIANA SMALL: Thanks for the willingness to collaborate. You should never stop writing. You have a gift.

TO THE CASTS OF RH, RHII, AND ECCLESIA: You spent hundreds of hours in rehearsal rooms, memorizing lines, training in weight rooms, developing your voices, discussing your spirituality, sharing yourselves. I consider every moment I spent with you a gift from God. You have been His instruments of love and grace in my life.

To the Off-Stage Crews of RH, RHII, and Ecclesia: You are the all-too-often-un-thanked foot soldiers that have made this play series possible. I am very grateful for the many, many hours you've dedicated to turning dreams into productions.

Josh Daneshforooz: Thank you for setting hearts into motion with an idea that stretches far beyond yourself. You are an inspirational figure with a prophetic vision…a dangerous combo.

Joyce Luy: Thank you for forcing me to ask myself what I really wanted out of my education. I am deeply grateful for our friendship.

Marla Kranick: Thank you for stopping me in the hallway to tell me about Westmont.

Mom and Dad: Dad, I owe you my managerial skill. Mom, I owe you the flat-out-or-stop passion. Thanks for your constant support, your belief in the vision, and for not asking the "what are you going to do with a theatre major" question too often.

Appendix B

Angel Writings

What follows are the original writings of the actors, based primarily on the scripture, but grown by their experience in this play. These words were spoken continuously as the audience entered. When the script, on page 1, refers to "Street prophets slamming down prayers," this is what it sounded like for us.

Angel 1
(Hayley Fulton)

Hope
In the beginning, for Adam, for Eve
Hope
For the promise of children like the stars
Hope
For a land of our own
Hope
For a future in You, Yahweh
Yae though I
Hope
With Elijah as he calls on Your fire
Hope
In the courage of Esther's foot steps
Hope
In Joseph's dreams
Hope
From the stone in David's Hand
Yea Though I Walk through the valley of the shadow of death I
Hope
For peace, prosperity, preservation in Your truth
Hope
For redemption of the oppressed for Your justice
Hope
For a generation of hearts bursting with Your love

Hope

For a future soaked in Your word

Hope

That it's not too late

I shall fear no evil because I

Hope

For every charred and scarlet sin

Hope

For each painful memory and open wound

Hope

For the empty and wandering souls

Hope

For unity

Hope

I've been forgiven blessed above being right

Hope for anointing

The Lord is my

Hope

In yourself when you hear His calling

Hope

To lead whoever is lost or broken

Hope

Like a prayer candle

Hope

For strength and the light

Hope

You can hear me can you hear me

Hope

For the poor in spirit

Hope

For they who mourn

Hope

For the meek

Hope

For they who hunger and thirst for righteousness

Hope

For the merciful

Hope

For the pure of heart

Hope

For the peacemakers

Hope

For they who are persecuted for the sake of

righteousness

Hope

like Isaiah

Hope

like Ezekiel

Hope

like Jeremiah

Hope

like Simeon

Hope

like a dream

He restoreth my

Hope

Angel 2

(Kellie Parkinson)

Curling smoke of incense lifts the prayers of the saints and I urge all to stillness: Listen to that which I am commanded to witness. Let everyone who has ears hear: the time is near.

Suffering in isolation, I have shattered the mirrors that once testified connection to my Creator. I can no longer find His image in the stranger of my reflection. My voice catches the fragments of glass that pin me to my knees. In the silence I hear again: the approach of the yet Unseen. To be judged or to be redeemed? Cowering in the wake of my own shadow, I crawl, beast-like into the night. The sudden vision pierces the dark and I am chained to light:

Again, a Voice, "The time is near."

Behold: He comes not in thunder nor in flame, nor in earthquakes nor in rain: But in Silence. He is that still, small voice penetrating the darkness. Whispers build in this place--mounting in elation, voices screaming their salvation, heralding this beginning of the end: the hour of testing; the hour that is to come upon the world. In this hour, the Church raises her head: the weary shoulders lift as she listens. Shuddering the approach of her Bridegroom, her eyes meet mine. In them I find the blood of prophets and of saints and of all who have been slain on earth. It pours from her tears, from her fingers, mingling with the blood at the feet of the trumpeted Lamb. That Lamb, the Thief, steals the night and all is light:

"The time is near."

Consuming fire burns not in pillars of rage but in quiet rivers, twisting tendrils around her outstretched arms. His whisper trickles through the flames, rising, falling with her breath at his feet. Air crackles in their meeting and in this place, I cloak my face yet I cannot tear my stare away: I hear Him say her name: the haunting voice heals her shame, and still she recoils in fear. Let everyone who has ears hear that whisper clear:

"The time is near."

Angel 3
(Ethan Warner)
Inspired by Daniel 7-8, Amos 8

Before me are the four winds of heaven,
churning up the great sea. Four great beasts, each one different,
coming up from the sea.

The first is a lion with wings of an eagle. Its wings were torn off and
its standing on two feet like a man.
The second beast arises, this one a bear with three bloody ribs in its mouth.

Next, a leopard. And on its back, four bird-like wings. This four-
headed leopard is being given authority to rule.

A fourth powerful beast is rising. This one more terrifying and
frightening than the others and very powerful. With its ten horns
and large iron teeth, it crushes
and devours. It stomps on whatever pieces of flesh are left.

"Thrones are set in place,
    and the Ancient of Days takes his seat.
  His clothing, white as snow;
       His hair, white like wool.
  His throne, flaming with fire,
  and its wheel, all ablaze.
A river of fire is flowing,
    coming out from before him.
    Thousands upon thousands attend him;
    ten thousand times ten thousand are standing before him.
    The court is seated,
    and the books are opened.

One like a Son of Man is coming with the clouds of heaven. He approaches the Ancient of Days and is being led into His presence. He is being given authority, glory and sovereign power; all peoples, nations and men of every language worship him. His dominion is an everlasting dominion that will not pass, and his kingdom will never be destroyed.' The saints of the Most High will receive the kingdom and will possess it Forever.'

The songs in the temple have become wailing wailing. Bodies are being flung everywhere! Silence!"

> Hear this, you who trample the needy
>   and do away with the poor of the land,
> You say
>   "When will the New Moon be over
>   so we may sell grain,
>   and when will the Sabbath be end
>   so we may market wheat?"

Your focus is on your work and not the Lord.

You boost the prices and cheat others with dishonest scales. You neglect the poor with by buying your silver and the needy for a pair of sandals.

The land trembles for these sins. All who live in it mourn. The whole land rises like the Nile. The Lord makes the sun go down at noon, and darkens the earth in broad daylight. He turns your religious feasts into mourning and all your singing into weeping. The Lord makes all of you wear sackcloth and shave your heads. The Lord sends a famine through the land. Not a famine of food or a thirst for water, but a famine of hearing the words of the LORD. The Lord is not speaking, because you are not listening.

Men stagger from sea to sea and wander from north to east, searching for the word of the LORD, but they will not find it. Lovely young women and strong young men faint because of thirst for His words.

Angel 4

(Andrew Massena)

I once heard the three prophets speak:
"I am going to bring my servant the Branch,
who will spring from the shoot
born out of the stump of Jesse.
I will raise him,
and he will become king,
the greatest yet seen,
and the greatest who will ever be."

That one the three prophets spoke of,
I saw, was Joshua,
the high priest of Israel,
who was dressed in filthy rags he called robes.

And the Lord commanded:
"Awake, O Sword, against my
                    shepherd, the Branch.
Kill the shepherd, so the sheep
                will scatter."

And it happened:
on high he hung, the Branch,
dead before the rotting earth,
holding each one's own in his heart.

Then I saw the Lord standing by the Branch,
saying to the angels nearby,
"Take off his filthy clothes."
And whispering to Branch, he said,
"Dying, you destroyed death.

Rising, you will restore life.
And so, arise! Arise!"
And the Branch, as if waking from sleep, arose.

Then the Lord commanded:
"Gather silver and gold and craft a crown.
Set it on the head of the high priest Joshua, the Branch:
for he will branch out to all people,
and he will construct the temple of the Lord."

Then I heard the Lord say:
"The time has come:
I will put my people into the fire,
like silver, purifying them,
like gold, testing them.
They will call on the name of the Lord,
> "Come rescue me!"

and I will save them.
I will say, 'You are my bride';
and they will say, "You are our groom,
our God."

Then the high priest Joshua will stand,
and at his right hand will be Satan, accusing him.
And the Lord will say to Satan,
"The Lord rebuke you, O Satan!
The Lord who has chosen Jerusalem rebuke you!
For the Branch who has come out of the fire is now pure."

Then the waters of life will flow from Jerusalem.
And the Branch will build the temple of the Lord;
and will rule from his throne.
And a priest will stand next to him,
in full communion with him.
Their hearts, and minds, and souls will be one.
People from far off will come
and help build the temple.
And the Lord will be king over the entire earth.
The Lord will be one and his name one.

Angel 5

(Ashley Myers)

Inspired by Ezekiel 2 and 16, Hosea 2

It happened to me
One day, as I was sitting on the beach
The surf shining like sea glass
His voice came
"Daughter"…he said
"Stand up and I will speak to you."
As he spoke the Spirit came into me and raised me to my feet
"Daughter, I am sending you to the church, to my Beloved
A rebellious deceitful body
The people I am sending you to are obstinate and stubborn.
Say to them….
This is what the Sovereign Lord says
And whether they listen, or shut their ears and fail to listen
They will know a prophet has spoken to them.
Do not be afraid of them or their words.
Open your mouth and eat what I give you."
Then I looked and a hand stretched out to me.
It held a scroll that unrolled. It was scripted with a story of love created and defiled
And he said to me,
"Daughter of man, eat what is before you
Eat this scroll, then go and speak to my bride."
So, I opened my mouth and ate it
It sat on my tongue, dissolving into sweet honey.
This is what the Sovereign Lord says
To his Bride, to his Church
"You, the church, the bride that was pure
The bride who wandered in the garden tucking scents into her garment,

Who dressed in white without hypocrisy
Whose lips were reserved for smoky prayers of incensed delight,
Whose eyes met the gaze of her beloved without shame,
That bride is gone."
"Who are you?
You revel in the destruction of the high places, roaming the refused mountain ranges
Building altars for your glory.
You sit atop these makeshift shrines, spreading your charms like silk cloth
Giving yourself to men who should be refused.
Drunk in your desires
You spill your seduction over those who pass, taking on new lovers.
You watch the pain of others,
Mocking their suffering, reveling in the blood that spills around you.
You claim compassion to be a mother to the needy and broken,
But you bar your arms in obstinacy;
Laughing at the homeless,
Refusing the motherless from your arms,
Spitting on the lost and broken.
You offer your own children to the gods of your imagination,
Who you gave power through distant prayers and bloody sacrifices,
Breathing evil breath into their hallow hearts of wood and stone."
"Listen, My beloved...
High on your walls the watchmen stand
They watch and wait, straining eyes and ears to see and hear the Word
To see the sword coming
They shout: Turn, turn, turn from your wicked ways
Will you listen? You will not
Like a petulant child you will shut your ears
You will spread your charms and spin webs of seduction again
Seducing yourself with your own lies..."
Church, listen
Remove the adulterous look from your face
And the unfaithfulness you hang as a charm between your breasts
He is coming, He will strip you naked, as bare as you were on the day you were born.
Your pools of charm, your beauty will wither and dry
You will harden like the desert, like a parched land
In your decrepit disintegration, you will try to go after your lovers
But he will block your path – He will wall you in

You will chase after you lovers and not find them
You will want to come back to him, your husband
But he says,
"First, because you have not acknowledged my gifts or love, I will strip you of everything, every art, every prosperity…until you have nothing…
Then
When you wear shame like a burlap cloak
When your eyes stream in remorse
When you cover the sores on your body, knowing they are signs of your debauchery
Then
I will allure you
I will lead you into the desert
And there, in your misery
When you think it is the end
I will speak tenderly to you
Then
I will give you back your beauty
I will give you back your prosperity
Your house will be a door of hope, you will sing the scented songs of your youth
Who is this coming from the east?
Garments stained crimson? Robed in splendor?
Striding forward in the greatness of his strength?
It is I
Speaking in righteousness mighty to save
Speaking of hope to you
And you will call me husband, lover, beloved, instead of master
And I will betroth you to me forever
In love and compassion
In faithfulness."

Angel 6

(Becky Thompson)

Inspired by Jeremiah 3 and 30

God looks at his children: "I wish I could take you back, give you the best land, the best of the inheritance. I thought you would call me 'Dad' again. But you walked out on me, like a woman cheating on her husband."

As God's saying this, voices come drifting, drifting from barren hilltops. It's God's children crying, weeping, pleading; weeping because they see their own perverted lives. They know they've been cheating on him.

Then God says, "Come back. I know you're faithless, but I'll cure you of that."

"Oh yes, please God, we'll come back to you! All that popular religion was just a cheap lie! – all those idols – but God! We know you're our only real hope! Look how the lies we've been living have devoured our inheritance: flocks, herds, sons, daughters – it's all gone! Just leave us to wallow in our shame! We've been cheating on you, and here you see us now in our own dirty sheets."

But again, God tells His children, "Come back. Just come back to me. Just leave those idols behind and stop wandering away from me. Circumcise yourselves to me. Cut away the foreskins of your hearts, that they might be soft for me. Otherwise, my wrath will break out, and my anger is like fire, a fire that can't be quenched. And that evil in your hearts is the fuel for my fire."

Oh, I see it – God's wrath – it's like a storm, bursting everywhere; a driving wind swirling down on the heads of those who disobey him. And it's not stopping. I can't describe it, but later you'll understand. You'll see it too, when God comes to reign.

But now He's telling His children that He's going to start over: "I'm starting over with you. I'm building you back up. Pick up your musical instruments; lets sing and dance together to celebrate! Sing with joy! Shout praises! I'm restoring your land, and soon you'll come to Zion to be with me on my holy mountain!"

I see God bringing His people back: blind, lame, children, pregnant women, old men – all coming back in a huge crowd. They're crying, weeping, praying but God's showing them where to walk: on level ground so they won't trip, and along a peaceful stream. God says, "See? My children scattered, but I'm gathering them up again."

Now they're at the mountain, and they're shouting and singing, and even dancing! There's so much food! – Plates and cups overflowing! God's filling his people with more than enough; His joy and His goodness satisfy.

Angel 7
Justin Davis

And the word of the Lord came to me. "Son of heaven. Set your face toward the sons of men, and deliver unto them the will of Elohim. Say unto them that this is what the Lord commands." For too long have men wallowed in their self pity, waiting for the day of the Lord to come upon them. Do you not know that that day has already come to pass? The spirit of the Lord has descended on the people and waits not for weary saints. Therefore go out, any among you. Go out and seek, and find the will of God in your life. Earnestly seek after what he has called you to do and you will be blessed with tongues of fire. With visions, and prayers, and spiritual giftings. You will be set apart among the nations as warriors who do battle on behalf of all mankind. As some have seen, the days of antiquity, of prophets and healers have indeed faded like the autumn leaves. But behold! The winter has passed and the end of days is fast approaching, the time has come once again for the Lord to raise up those among you who are willing to be his hands and mouth. Sons of men I speak to you on behalf of Him who has sent me! Be sober, be vigilant, take up your cross and defend your calling. Speak the truth to the nations of things that have not yet come to pass! Give hope to the hopeless, hear the cries of the weak and go to their rescue! Speak on their behalf in words they cannot hear with effectual fervency as you have been commanded! For your brothers are fruitless, and are all but withered and dead! Breathe new life into this broken world as it has been set forth long before this day. For this is the will of the Father.

"This is the word of the Lord spoken unto you for His sovereign purpose."

Sword, spears, guns and blasts.

The day of the Lord is fast approaching.

Who among you will hear the will of the father,
    and be strengthened by the might of the holy one?
Who among you will learn his gifts for the kingdom,
    and live out and practice in blind expectation?
Who will lead in the truth and step out from their kin,
    to say Jesus is nowhere behind these lips?
Who will stand alone in the realm of angels
    that he may speak to his brethren of the battle still raging?

The day of the Lord is fast approaching.

I see a man who dismisses his scripture,
what he is commanded draws too much attention.
I see a woman engulfed in tears,
for the first time she feels a total surrender.
I see a boy with a heart pure as crystal,
he knows God is bigger than his biggest sin.
I see a girl whose prayers fall on deaf ears,
Her heart has been perverted by glimmering things.

The day of the Lord is fast approaching.

And when that day comes...

All at once the earth will shake, the seas will roar the ground will open up, The dead will rise, the living will die, the powers that be will flee for their lives. The innocent will be raised up, the guilty will see their day of reckoning, the children will leave their mothers and fathers and join with those who still hold the truth. The plants and animals and rocks will cry out for the outpouring of justice. And as this great equilibrium is superseded with truth, all will be made right for a time, as the world loses to the thing it has tried hardest to kill.

Appendix C

Design Sketches
(Matthew Jones)

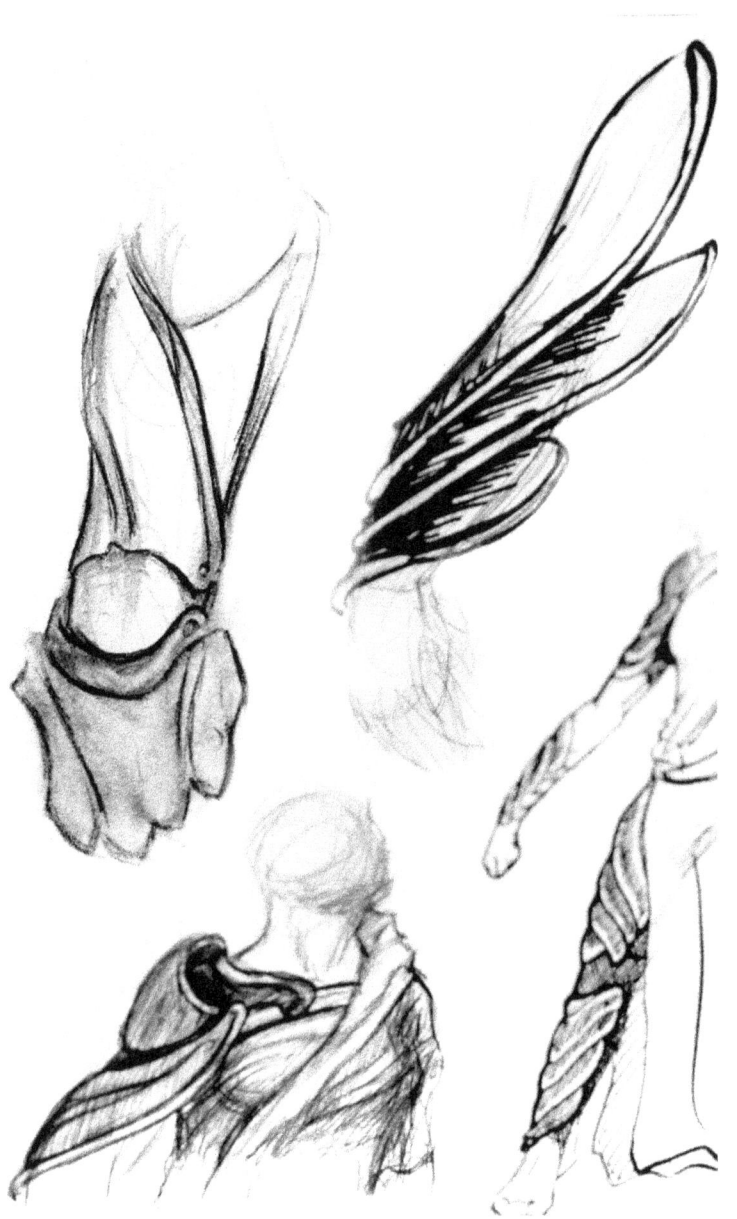

Appendix D

Suggested Reading

Here are a few books that significantly informed this production of *Ecclesia*. They come with the highest recommendation and provide an excellent window into where the play received its...

THEOLOGY

Barron, Robert. *And Now I See: A Theology of Transformation*
Barron, Robert. *The Strangest Way: Walking the Christian Path*
L'Engle, Madeline. *Walking on Water: Reflections on Faith and Art*
Claiborne, Shane. *The Irresistible Revolution*

THEATRICALITY

Bogart, Anne and Tina Landau. *The Viewpoints Book: A Practical Guide to Viewpoints and Composition*
Bogart, Anne. *A Director Prepares: Seven Essays on Art in Theatre*
Schechner, Richard. *Environmental Theatre*

WRITING STYLE

Ehn, Erik. *The Saint Plays*
Eliot, T. S. *Murder in the Cathedral*

www.ingramcontent.com/pod-product-compliance
Lightning Source LLC
Chambersburg PA
CBHW071313040426
42444CB00009B/2003